Water
Everywhere!

Written by Christine Taylor-Butler   **Illustrated by Maurie J. Manning**

Children's Press®
A Division of Scholastic Inc.
New York • Toronto • London • Auckland • Sydney
Mexico City • New Delhi • Hong Kong
Danbury, Connecticut

To Ken, Alexis, and Olivia,
with special thanks to Robert, Audrey, and Eileen R.
— C.T.B.

With love to Shire, from her fairy godmother
— M.J.M.

Consultant

Eileen Robinson
Reading Specialist

Library of Congress Cataloging-in-Publication Data

Taylor-Butler, Christine.
  Water everywhere! / written by Christine Taylor-Butler ;
illustrated by Maurie J. Manning.
      p. cm. — (A Rookie reader)
  Summary: A young child describes some of the many ways water is used.
  ISBN 0-516-25153-8 (lib. bdg.)   0-516-25285-2 (pbk.)
  [1. Water—Fiction.] I. Manning, Maurie, ill. II. Title. III. Series.
  PZ7.B9785Wat 2004
  [E]—dc22
                              2004009324

CHILDREN'S PRESS, and A ROOKIE READER®, and associated logos are trademarks
and or registered trademarks of Scholastic Library Publishing. SCHOLASTIC and
associated logos are trademarks and or registered trademarks of Scholastic Inc.
1 2 3 4 5 6 7 8 9 10 R 14 13 12 11 10 09 08 07 06 05

It's morning!
Time to start my day.

I wash my face before I play.

I brush my teeth in the sink.

I give my lizard fresh water to drink.

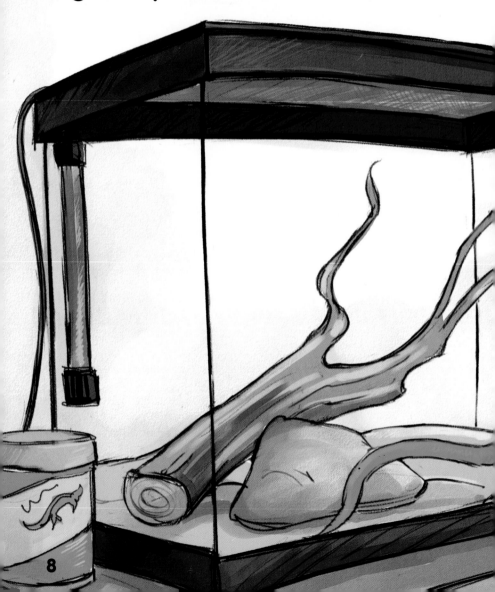

I make a batch of lemonade.

I put flowers in the vase I made.

I make rainbows with
the garden hose.

I watch the clouds.
What shapes are those?

Uh oh! I feel raindrops.

I splash in every puddle around.

I see my reflection on the ground.

24

I come inside and fill the tub.

I make lots of bubbles.
Time to scrub.

I'd still be out if not for the rain.

Tomorrow I will start again.

Word List (72 Words)

a	face	it's	put	time
again	feel	lemonade	rain	to
and	fill	lizard	rainbows	tomorrow
are	flowers	lots	raindrops	tub
around	for	made	reflection	uh
batch	fresh	make	scrub	vase
be	garden	morning	see	wash
before	give	my	shapes	watch
brush	ground	not	sink	water
bubbles	hose	of	splash	what
clouds	I	oh	start	will
come	I'd	on	still	with
day	if	out	teeth	
drink	in	play	the	
every	inside	puddle	those	

About the Author

Christine Taylor-Butler studied both engineering and art and design at the Massachusetts Institute of Technology. She's an explorer at heart and loves playing in the water. When she's not writing stories for children, you'll find her buried in her mountain of books. She lives in Kansas City, Missouri, with her husband, two daughters, and her pride of black cats!

About the Illustrator

Maurie J. Manning's illustrations first appeared in the 1960s on the end pages of the books in her parent's library. Since then, she has learned that drawing in other peoples' books is not allowed and that it's better to make your own books. She is the author and illustrator of a 2004 International Reading Association's Notable Book, and has illustrated many other books. She lives in Southern California with her two children, where they enjoy water very much.